Original title:
Roots and Resilience

Copyright © 2025 Creative Arts Management OÜ
All rights reserved.

Author: Tobias Sterling
ISBN HARDBACK: 978-1-80567-399-6
ISBN PAPERBACK: 978-1-80567-698-0

Unyielding Foundations

In my garden, weeds do dance,
But my veggies, they take a stance.
With a twist, they sway and prance,
In a salad bowl, they'll take a chance.

The carrots tell jokes from below,
While potatoes steal the show.
Laughing at the thunder's grow,
'Bring it on!' they start to glow.

Tides of Tenacity

The ocean waves may pull and shove,
Yet the crabs find the space to shove.
With tiny claws, they show their love,
Beneath the foam, like a gentle glove.

In every splash, there's a strong cheer,
The fish wiggle, "We have no fear!"
Dodging nets and bubbles near,
Their antics make it all too clear.

Bonds in the Soil

Worms in the ground are quite the crew,
Organizing dirt balls with a view.
"You dig it, I'll carry, just me and you!"
In a compost heap, they start to brew.

The daisies gossip, gossip loud,
"Look at that! A sunflower proud!"
In this earth, they're never cowed,
Sharing secrets of the crowd.

Echoes of the Past

Old trees whisper tales of yore,
Of squirrels dancing, never a bore.
They chuckle at the kids galore,
Playing tag 'round trunks, SO much more!

And when the wind starts to play loud,
The branches wobble, feeling proud.
"Remember when we swayed so proud?"
Nature's humor, a joyful crowd.

Surviving Through Seasons

Winter's bite, I wear my coat,
The snowmen march, but I stay afloat.
Spring arrives with pollen's cheer,
I sneeze three times, drink ginger beer.

Sunshine blares, I hide in shade,
Ice cream melts while I parade.
Leaves then fall, I check my shoes,
Autumn's here, but I refuse to lose.

The Unbreakable Bond.

You stole my fries, oh what a crime,
But we still laugh, it feels just fine.
Falling out? That's not our way,
In silly fights, we're here to stay.

You call me names, I roll my eyes,
Yet in our trouble, we both rise.
With goofy jokes and stories wild,
We keep our friendship, forever styled.

Beneath the Surface

In puddles deep, I take a leap,
Splashing gently, the laughs I keep.
Fish swim by with curious grins,
Beneath the waves, we all are kin.

The current sways, I twirl around,
Water's dance, I won't be drowned.
With floating dreams and silly sighs,
I'm anchored here, beneath the skies.

Strength in the Shadows

In corners dark, my secret laughs,
A dance with shadows, the sweetest gaffes.
When life is tough, I crack a joke,
In every glum, I see a poke.

Between the lines, a giggle sings,
Jokes from nowhere, like rubber springs.
Don't fear the night, it's just a game,
You'll find me here, staying the same.

The Beauty Beneath

There's beauty in the dirt we tread,
Like socks and sandals wed,
A garden nestled deep below,
Where laughter blooms and veggies grow.

With roots that tickle, tease, and twist,
They plot their schemes, they can't resist,
While moles hold dance parties underground,
And worms keep grooving all around.

Rise from the Depths

From muck and mire, we spring anew,
Like ducks in tutus, don't ask who,
We strut our stuff with muddy feet,
   And pirouette to our own beat.

So when the skies unleash their tears,
We'll dance with glee and shed our fears,
For every puddle's just a stage,
   Where we perform, a wacky mage.

Unyielding Spirits

When life throws shade and clouds roll in,
We pop up heads with goofy grins,
Like dandelions in a tux,
We blossom proud, despite the flux.

With every storm that tries to squash,
We leave behind a funny swash,
With roots that won't give up the ghost,
And laughter's what we love the most.

Flourishing Against the Odds

In cracks of sidewalks, we defy,
With tiny flowers reaching high,
A sprout in sneakers leaps for joy,
Outshining doom like a fab ploy.

For every blunder, we will cheer,
A comedy of growth, oh dear,
With seedlings strutting through the haze,
Dancing through life in quirky ways.

Echoes in the Stillness

In the garden, weeds throw a party,
They dance and sway, oh so hearty.
The flowers frown, they throw shade,
"Why can't they learn?" a sunflower brayed.

Beneath a rock, a worm is wise,
He grins at storms, with squinty eyes.
"Life's a wiggle, not a fight!"
He doing the salsa, oh what a sight!

Mice gather 'round, a comedy show,
"Who knew grass grew on a dough?"
They laugh so hard, they spill their seeds,
In nature's fun, all plant life leads.

With roots all tangled, they joke and jest,
"We're stronger together, that's our quest!"
In their little world, they thrive and laugh,
Turning struggles into a hearty gaff.

Sentinels of Strength

Tall trees flex as the wind blows by,
"I can bend, but I'll never cry!"
The branches sway and twist about,
"Try to uproot me? What a clout!"

Squirrels giggle, premiers of pranks,
"We're the kings!" they proudly flanked.
They leap from trunk to trunk with glee,
"Catch me if you can!" chirps a tree.

Old stones chuckle as the river knits,
"We've seen it all, through all kinds of fits!"
They watch the water laugh and swirl,
"No rock can stop us!" they grin and whirl.

With nature's antics, they find delight,
Every twist and turn, a laugh ignites.
In this great play, they need no cue,
United in joy, both old and new.

Nature's Comrade

The bumblebee buzzes a silly tune,
"I'll pollinate under the moon!"
While daisies giggle in the sun,
They raise their petals, joining the fun.

A chubby caterpillar does a roll,
"I'll spin a cocoon, it's my goal!"
The butterflies wish him all the best,
"Just don't forget, we love a jest!"

Ants line up, in a perfect row,
Organized chaos, but they steal the show.
With tiny helmets, they march and cheer,
"No crumbs left behind, that's our frontier!"

Among the trees, a gentle tease,
"Hey, oak! That's quite the sneeze!"
With laughter ringing through the leaves,
Nature's crew just loves to believe.

Unfurling Amidst Strife

In the midst of chaos, a sprout appears,
With a cheeky grin, it laughs at fears.
"Though life's a tussle, I'll take a chance,"
It wiggles and jigs, initiating a dance.

A tulip quips, "I'm a diva, you see,
Even through storms, I sway with glee!"
While raindrops giggle on my head,
"I'll bloom for sunshine!" it sweetly said.

Dandelions blow wishes to the breeze,
"Come join our party, we do as we please!"
They float carefree, no worries in sight,
Transforming the mundane to pure delight.

In the wild, laughter weaves through the air,
With every challenge, they learn to share.
In this playful realm, where all intertwine,
Life's little joys are simply divine.

Tethered to Tomorrow

In the garden of dreams we stumble,
With toy balloons that pop and tumble.
We trip on weeds, but laugh instead,
Each snappy quip, a wink to dread.

A tree in flip-flops, dancing around,
Waving to squirrels who gather 'round.
They play charades in shadows cast,
As time flies by, so quick, so fast.

We sing to clouds that seem confused,
"Are we all nuts?!" we jovially muse.
A farmer's hat sits on a cat,
As if it's royal—oh, how we chat!

So here's to hope in all its forms,
That brings us joy through raging storms.
With laughter's gift, we find our way,
Tomorrow's bright—a giggling play!

Flowers in the Ashes

From burnt remains, a daisy pokes,
It whispers, "Life is but a hoax!"
A cackle from the embers glows,
"Let's dance on ashes, strike silly poses!"

A phoenix sneezes, bursts in flames,
"Oops! Sorry folks, just playing games!"
While fireflies joke, "We're just the sparks,
Creating laughter in the dark!"

Shoes of smoke, with soles of cheer,
Skip through the fire, cast off your fear.
In every charred and broken place,
A laugh erupts—oh, what a space!

So let's toss seeds where laughter grows,
In places where no one ever goes.
A riot of color, wild and sweet,
In chaos and laughter, life's a treat!

Beneath the Surface

A fish in glasses swims with flair,
Winks at the cat lounging in a chair.
"Just look at those humans below,
Making waves, putting on a show!"

Bubbles giggle, tickling the sea,
"Let's bubble-wrap some silliness, whee!"
The octopus juggles clam-and-sand,
"Join the circus, it's all quite grand!"

With starfish clapping flippery claps,
They plot and scheme in their underwater laps.
A crab in a tux holds up a sign,
"Ebb and flow, sip your brine!"

In tidal twists and turns so wide,
Laughter swells, we roll with tide.
So let's dive deep, enjoy the play,
Embrace the splash—we float away!

Strands of Solace

In tangled locks, we find some fun,
A hairpin dodges, no need to run.
A ribbon giggles, twirling in air,
"Welcome to chaos, if you dare!"

Comb a little doubt, let reason fray,
A snip of laughter lights the way.
With every strand, we braid a song,
In messy knots, we can't go wrong!

A brush with humor, unkempt and wild,
In the garden of care, we're always a child.
"So much potential in every twist,
Let's dance with folly, we shall persist!"

So weave your tale, let colors soar,
With every giggle, we're bound for more.
Within each twist, life's laughter shines,
In playful knots, our spirit aligns!

Grit in the Garden

In the soil, I dig my toes,
Planting dreams where laughter grows.
Weeds may mock, but I don't care,
I'll dance with dirt, a true debonair.

Sunshine sprinkles on my hat,
While grasshoppers giggle—a chatty brat.
I shout, "Grow tall!" to every sprout,
A comedic scene, can't turn about.

Worms wiggle, thinking they're slick,
But I'm the one who knows the trick.
With every seed, I tease the ground,
In my silly garden, joy is found.

Bunnies stealing my carrot prize,
I chase them off with clownish cries.
In this patch where jests take flight,
It's grit that makes the fun so bright.

Waves of Fortitude

The ocean roars with a giggly wave,
A jellyfish wearing a crinkled rave.
I'll surf my fears on a wobbly board,
While seagulls dip like a strange accord.

With every splash, I stand up tall,
Pretending I'm not scared of the fall.
The tide may tease, but I just grin,
Catching joy like seaweed in a spin.

Crabs parade in a sideways dance,
While I attempt my silliest prance.
Ocean spray in my hair blurs the view,
But laughter echoes, it's all that I knew.

Riding storms like a quirky vehicle,
Turning mishaps into the most comical.
In this sea of chuckles, come what may,
Fortitude dances like it's on display.

Threads of Lasting Hope

In my closet, a tapestry hides,
Made of mismatched socks and funky strides.
I stitch together dreams with flair,
Each thread a giggle, ironies we share.

Unraveled seams? No need to stress,
They just add to my patchwork mess.
With every pull, I weave a grin,
Knitting up joy from yarn and kin.

Buttons bouncing like a cheerful crowd,
As I flaunt my coat, oh so loud.
With patches of laughter 'neath every seam,
My quirky quilt is the ultimate dream.

A fabric of fun, stitched with delight,
Colors colliding in pure insight.
For though life may tear, we won't mope,
In every stitch, we find our hope.

Life's Quiet Triumphs

Sipping tea while the world spins fast,
Celebrating moments, making them last.
A forgotten dance in my kitchen space,
With the broom as my partner, a silly grace.

I trip on a sock, it's a comedic show,
As I twirl like a leaf in the autumn's flow.
Every tumble, I chuckle, no need to hide,
Finding joy in the little, it's a glorious ride.

A puzzle piece missing? Oh, what a tease!
But I smile and giggle, it's all just a breeze.
In the chaos of life, we find the serene,
Triumph is laughing, it's not what it seems.

So here's to the quirks, a wink at the fate,
In every quiet win, we creatively celebrate.
With hearts light as feathers, we carry the light,
In this zoo of existence, it's all about delight.

Deep Anchors

In the garden, gnomes do dance,
While plants conspire, given a chance.
With every sprout, they make a pact,
Together they'll form a leafy act.

Down below, the worms do cheer,
Their underground parties bring good cheer.
Wiggling through, they're nature's crew,
Making sure the greens are due.

Sun above, with cheeky rays,
Winks and laughs throughout the days.
While down below, the salad sings,
Raising up their leafy wings.

So here's a toast, to silly greens,
With roots that hide and dance in scenes.
For all the joy that nature brings,
Let's celebrate with all our things!

From Earth to Sky

Up in the trees, the squirrels conspire,
Chasing each other in branches higher.
Spinning tales of acorn hoards,
Their chatter echoing like silly chords.

Caterpillars don their best parade,
Gossiping of dreams, in leaves they've laid.
While ants march by with a tiny shout,
"Keep it moving, no time to pout!"

Clouds float by in a fluffy race,
While breezes tickle each leafy face.
The sun shines bright, encouraging pranks,
As nature fulfils her wild antics banks.

Celebrate the chaos, let laughter fly,
With nature's whims from earth to sky.
For every giggle, every twist and bend,
Shows how even sprouts can ascend!

The Strength Beneath

Beneath the ground, where secrets hide,
Little potatoes grin with pride.
"Look at us!" they shout out loud,
"We're the stars of every foodie crowd!"

The mushrooms bloom with hats so bright,
Throwing parties deep in the night.
"Who knew being damp could be such fun?
Join us now, we've just begun!"

As roots twist and twirl, they share their tales,
Of epic storms and endless gales.
"Did you hear about that last rainstorm?
We danced in puddles, kept so warm!"

Let's cheer for the life that grows below,
In muddy patches where laughter flows.
For beneath it all, there's always mirth,
In this wild and wondrous earth!

Whispers of the Ancients

In the wind, the old trees laugh,
Telling tales of a silly path.
"Remember when we dodged that storm?
We shook our leaves, despite the norm!"

Squirrels gather, taking notes,
Munching acorns, wearing coats.
With every tale that's passed around,
They hop and bounce upon the ground.

Each twig and branch a memory holds,
Of mischief born and adventures bold.
"Don't forget the time we played pretend,
When winter froze, but we would blend!"

So here's to stories, old and wise,
That bubble up like sweet surprise.
For in each whisper lies the cheer,
Of ancient laughter that draws us near!

Hearts in the Underbrush

In the thicket where the wild things play,
A squirrel lost his acorn today.
He searched with a frown, oh what a sight,
While singing a song that was quite tight.

Under bushes, in patches of green,
He danced like a fool, quite unseen.
With each little stumble, he thought it was grand,
Finding joy in the mess, wasn't life just planned?

Through nettles and thorns, he wiggled with glee,
Twirling around like a jigging flea.
A wily old fox joined in the spree,
Together they laughed, wild and carefree.

So if you find trouble, do give a laugh,
With friends by your side, it's a comical path.
For even in hardship, we flourish and thrive,
Like a squirrel on a quest, oh how we survive!

The Gritty Harvest

Farmer Joe had a patch that was grand,
Carrots and radishes growing like planned.
He tripped on his hoe, fell right in the mud,
And sprang back up, looking like a big bud.

"Veggies aren't growing, they're just having fun!"
He chuckled aloud, blinking at the sun.
His cabbage rolled over, gave a leafy sigh,
As he tried to coax it, "Don't let dreams die!"

With a basket of greens and a wink in his eye,
He'd trade 'em for pies, oh me, oh my!
But when he looked deeper, he found a delight,
A pumpkin who giggled, "I'm ready for night!"

In harvesting laughter, he reaped more than yield,
Each veggie a buddy, each field a fair field.
So when crops seem tough, keep the chuckles alive,
For the grit of the soil makes the best dreams thrive!

A Symphony of Endurance

In a garden of chaos, a cat made a band,
With carrots for drums, and a stick in his hand.
The tomatoes were singing, oh what a scene,
As the lettuce did a waltz, like a leafy machine.

The radishes blushed, trying hard to play light,
While peas went rolling, just out of sight.
"The more, the merrier!" the cat gave a cheer,
As the worms formed a chorus that tickled the ear.

Even the weeds joined, much to their surprise,
Swaying and twirling under sunny skies.
Each scruffy note brought giggles galore,
A symphony made with roots galore!

So if life gets messy, just dance in the dirt,
With laughter and friends, let the worries convert.
For every small struggle, a song will unfold,
Bringing joy in the turmoil, like treasures of gold!

Footprints in the Earth

Little feet pitter-pat on the ground,
A dance of sweet mischief, chaos unbound.
They trace silly circles, then zigzag away,
Leaving prints that proclaim, "We're here to stay!"

In puddles and mud, they skip with great flair,
While squishing lost snails, and giggling in air.
Each step is a journey through stories untold,
With laughter the compass, more precious than gold.

As the sun dipped low, shadows began to play,
The footprints turned funky, like kids on parade.
With the stars shining bright, accepting the flair,
The earth held their footprints, a memory rare.

So let laughter guide your whimsical roam,
Through fields and adventures, where sunshine feels home.
With every small footprint making room for a cheer,
Life's dance in the soil brings the heart ever near!

Beneath the Weight of Stone

Underneath the mighty rock,
A snail's thoughts begin to flock.
"Why must I carry all this weight?"
"I just wanted to be first-rate!"

With every inch, a new complaint,
"This load, dear friends, it ain't quaint!"
But laugh they do, at nature's jest,
A snail's slow pace, a silly quest.

Through mud and muck, they slip and slide,
"Why not just ride the turtle tide?"
Yet still they plod, with shells so proud,
Creating smiles, a snaily crowd.

So next time you find burdens stark,
Remember the snail, and give a hark!
For life's a laugh, in snail's own way,
Heavy or light, let humor sway.

Lifting the Burden

An ant with weight of dinner rolls,
Dreams of lifting with its goals.
"I must outdo that lifting champ!"
"But first, a snack – I need a lamp!"

Its buddies cheer, "You can do it!"
While munching crumbs, they start to split.
"If we all push and lift as one,"
"Then we can have some real fun!"

They gather close, with tiny strength,
And lift that load with perfect length.
But then it tips, oh what a sight!
Dinner rolls take off in flight!

So if you feel that weight too great,
Remember joy can shift your fate.
Let laughter lift what bears you down,
With friends around, you'll never frown.

Anchors of Hope

In a garden tall, a weed stands proud,
"Why am I here?" it cries out loud.
"All around are blooms so bright,"
"Yet here's my fate, to never take flight!"

But then a bug sings in the air,
"You've got grit, you've got flair!"
"Anchored down in soil so deep,"
"You've got the strength; it's yours to keep!"

The bug points out each mighty feat,
"You don't need petals; you're still a treat!"
The weed chuckles, "I may be odd,
But truth be told, I am quite a god!"

So blooms rejoice with potent cheer,
For in odd places, hope draws near.
Just like the weeds that stand tall and cope,
Life's little quirks inspire hope.

Unseen Endurance

Beneath the soil, a worm does squirm,
Hidden from view, it's on a term.
"What's all the fuss with sun and light?"
"I make my path with pure delight!"

With little boots, it drills away,
"Tomorrow's party's what I say!"
A dance of dirt, a jig in grime,
Underground, it's always prime time.

A friend pops in, a toad so spry,
"Why work so hard when you can fly?"
The worm just smiles, as it gets around,
"I'm happy here, underground I'm crowned!"

So cheer for those who thrive unseen,
In every nook, life's like a dream.
For in the dirt, there's laughter spun,
In every wiggle, a ton of fun!

Grit of the Earth

In the garden, bugs do groan,
Spuds are rolling, seeds are sewn.
With muddy feet, I slip and slide,
Yet still, I bounce, and take in stride.

Worms throw parties, quite the scene,
While daisies dance, bright and green.
I try to plant my thoughts of flight,
But peas just laugh — they take delight!

The sun has smiles, the clouds will wink,
A carrot's stuck, but won't we think?
Through dirt and giggles, we shall play,
It's a rooty, tooty, fun-filled day!

So here's to joy, in every elbow,
A veggie dance, come join the show!
Though storms may come, we'll laugh it off,
In muddy mirth, we'll never scoff.

Whispers of the Underground

Down below, where critters chatter,
A tiny mouse yells, 'What's the matter?'
Rabbits giggle, groundhogs cheer,
As pancakes flip from roots so dear.

The radish whispers, 'Life is sweet!'
While turnips gossip, feeling neat.
A sunflower dreams of wearing shoes,
While dreaming of dancing, she'll make the news!

Together they plot, a gala grand,
With dandelions taking the stand.
They'll show the world their funny grace,
And leave all worries without a trace.

In the underground, there's quite a fuss,
As laughter flows, without a fuss.
So here we raise a toast to cheer,
To underground friends, we hold so dear!

Unbreakable Bonds

Together we sprout, like flowers in spring,
With laughter so loud, we dance and sing.
Silly little weeds in a flower brigade,
Hopping and bopping, in sun and shade.

The squash is shy, with a tiny grin,
While carrots can't stop from breaking in.
They joke and laugh about the tall weeds,
Comparing lives and all their needs.

Bouncing in rows, the peas all rhyme,
While tomatoes tell tales, passing time.
With roots intertwined, like friends at play,
They thrive on joy, come what may.

So here's our gift, as seasons pass,
A garden of giggles, a verdant mass.
In this patch of glee, we find our truth,
In friendships strong, we bask in youth.

Ties That Ground Us

In tangled knots, we form a crew,
With puns and laughter, oh so true.
The weeds declare, 'We're all for fun!'
While sunflowers claim they shine like the sun.

Old oaks have tales of the stormy nights,
While squirrels add humor with their antics, in flights.
Together we hold, through thick and thin,
As laughter echoes where we begin.

A family of ferns, with arms held high,
Embracing the wind, reaching for the sky.
Through hiccups and stumbles, we bounce back,
With silly grins, we're on the right track.

So let's celebrate this quirky crew,
With roots like ours, there's not much we can't do.
In life's funny garden, we flourish and thrive,
With ties that bind, we're so alive!

Invisible Ties

In a garden of socks, under the bed,
The lost ones giggle, all snug in their spread.
They twirl and they dance, a colorful crew,
Chasing dust bunnies, with mischief anew.

A tree in the yard, with a beard made of moss,
Whispers sweet secrets, as we toss and toss.
The wind makes a joke, leaves laugh in delight,
While squirrels debate, who gets the last bite.

Neighbors stare wide, at the antics we cheer,
As we wiggle our toes, in our laughter, sincere.
With each silly spill, like a dance on the ground,
We tumble and roll, till we're dizzy, unbound.

So here's to the threads, that bind us in glee,
To the socks and the trees, to you and to me.
In this humorous jumble, we thrive and we play,
Under sunshine and giggles, come what may.

Beneath the Weight

A coffee cup stained, like a raccoon's disguise,
Hiding the truth, with its sloshing good lies.
It brims with the weight of a tired old plot,
Where dreams take a nap, and solutions are sought.

The cat, with a smirk, steals the chair once so grand,
Claiming the throne, with a soft, furry hand.
While we juggle our woes, like oranges in air,
The universe laughs, at our bumbling care.

We waddle through life, in our mismatched shoes,
Each step a new chance to embrace or to lose.
The weight of it all, makes us wobble and sway,
Like balancing pancakes on a sunny day.

So we'll laugh through the load, this circus routine,
With pancakes and coffee, life's messy cuisine.
Beneath every burden, there's giggles to find,
As we waddle on by, with the world so unlined.

Clutching the Earth

A potato parade, rolling down from the hill,
With eyes wide open, they dance for the thrill.
They wriggle and hop, like they're late for a date,
While we giggle and cheer, 'Oh, it's never too late!'

The weeds are our friends, as they tug on our shoes,
Whispering tales of what not to refuse.
In gardens of chaos, we plant seeds of cheer,
With trowels like swords, we conquer our fear.

The earth gives a chuckle, as we muddle about,
With dirt on our noses, we're laughing, no doubt.
In the mess of it all, we find our true worth,
Clutching the ground, in our joyful rebirth.

So let's dance with our veggies, and jive with the soil,
In this goofy routine, let's dance and let's toil.
Together we flourish, in this wacky embrace,
With laughter and love, we reclaim our place.

Spiraling Through Time

A rubber band snaps, like a time-travel twist,
Sending us flying, through moments we've missed.
With laughter like music, it stretches so wide,
And pulls us together, like a carnival ride.

The clock plays its tricks, with its tick-tock refrain,
While we juggle our jellybeans, feeling no pain.
Each second that passes, brings giggles anew,
As we race with the shadows, beneath skies so blue.

We tumble and spiral, through ages of fun,
A parade of odd phrases, that never quite run.
With echoes of laughter, we bop through the years,
While time takes a break, rolling on with our cheers.

So here's to the journey, the quirkiness found,
In the spirals of life, we're all tightly bound.
With laughter as currency, we spin and we shine,
In this whimsical world, we dance through time.

Courageous Growth

In a garden where veggies think they're tough,
A carrot said, "I'll show them my stuff!"
With a wiggle and jive, it danced with glee,
While the potatoes just stared, "What a sight to see!"

A bean sprout declared, "I'm growing so high!"
While the lettuce chuckled, "Oh please, oh my!"
With a splash of sunshine and good old rain,
These veggies know comfort, but not the pain!

When the winds came howling, loud and bold,
The sprouts held hands, acting so bold.
Their roots entwined, in silly embrace,
They laughed at the storms, "This is our space!"

So if you feel shaky, just wiggle and sway,
Remember those veggies, come what may.
Life's a garden, a quirky old scene,
With a dash of humor, we'll keep it green!

The Heart's Resilience

A heart once wore a giant brass plate,
Claiming, "I'm tough, I just can't wait!"
But when love danced in with a silly grin,
The heart fell flat, but didn't chagrin.

With each tiny crack, it giggled and shook,
"Look at my splinters, I'm quite the book!"
While others would sigh, feeling quite sad,
The heart just responded, "I'm not so bad!"

When heartbreak knocked with its heavy boots,
"Ah, let's throw a party!" the heart just hoots.
It gathered the pieces, a colorful mess,
Said, "Let's mix them up, in our own fest!"

So here's to the heart that's crazy and wild,
Laughing at life, an eternal child.
With every patch, it shines like a star,
Nothing can stop it, no matter how far!

Branches Against the Storm

In a forest where trees gossip and sway,
A branch yelled, "Hold on, it's windy today!"
A neighbor replied, with a giggle so spry,
"Better dance with the breeze, or just say goodbye!"

When thunder rumbled, they donned little hats,
"Who needs umbrellas? We're not scared of bats!"
With a shake and a wiggle, they all joined the tune,
Even the roots tapped, 'neath the light of the moon.

"Let's have a party!" the branches all sang,
"But watch for the lightning, zap-zap, it's a bang!"
They twisted and turned, a festive ballet,
Laughing at raindrops, "It's our holiday!"

When the storm left town, with a whirl and a puff,
The branches stood proud, saying, "We're tough enough!"

Together they learned, with joy in their hearts,
Life's just a dance, and we're all works of art!

Through Cracks We Rise

A sidewalk took pride in its perfect old cracks,
Said, "Look at my style, no need for setbacks!"
The little weeds chuckled, sprouting so bold,
"We've grown in your gaps, it's a sight to behold!"

When the sun hit just right, they threw a grand spree,
"Join us, oh flowers, come dance with the bee!"
With laughter and colors, they sang through the day,
"Who said we're too small? We'll steal the whole play!"

The pavement rolled eyes, shook a little in pride,
"Here in these cracks, look at all of you slide!"
The whimsical crew, both sprightly and small,
Said, "Together we'll rise, we're having a ball!"

So when life gets tough, and you feel confined,
Remember those cracks, let your spirit unwind.
Find joy in the journey, let laughter set sail,
Together we flourish, we'll surely prevail!

Legacy of the Ancestors

In grandpa's tales of yore,
A chicken danced on the floor.
He swore it was true,
Just ask Aunt Lou!

With every big fish that got away,
He'd claim he caught it, hip hip hooray!
In the family tree,
Was a gnarled old bee!

When grandma baked pies with a wink,
They often came out pink!
A recipe bold,
More magic than gold!

So here's to the quirks of the past,
Where laughter flows and shadows cast.
These tales we share,
Make funny bones flare!

Echoes of the Past

In dusty corners, whispers call,
Of granddad's dance at the wall.
He spun like a top,
Till he took a flop!

The family photos all frown,
They wear the same goofy crown.
A smile so wide,
They couldn't hide!

Old Uncle Joe with his wobbly hat,
In a three-piece suit that was way too flat.
He'd strut and prance,
Barely keep his stance!

So here's to the echoes we find,
They jiggle and jive in our mind.
Let laughter ring,
In the joy they bring!

Through the Thorns

With every prick, we break a grin,
Who knew thorns could be where fun begins?
Amidst the snags,
We find laughing tags!

A hedgehog's waddle invites a cheer,
When caught in a thicket, we don't shed a tear.
In nature's jest,
We're simply blessed!

Through the twists and tangle we joke,
With giggles shared, our hearts invoke.
A twist and a turn,
For laughter we yearn!

So let's embrace every twist and turn,
For in the laughter, our hearts will burn.
Through all the strife,
We dance in life!

Lifelines in the Dark

In whispers soft, the night unfolds,
With tales of bold that never grows old.
A lantern glows,
As laughter flows!

Through shadowy paths, we trip and slide,
With friends who giggle and take it in stride.
When we get lost,
The joy's worth the cost!

In the midnight hour, ghostly sounds,
We share our secrets with giggly bounds.
With every jump,
We dodge the bump!

So here's to the light that guides our way,
With funny moments that come to play.
In the darkest night,
Laughter shines bright!

A Journey from Below

Beneath the ground with worms we play,
They laugh and wiggle all the way.
With every twist in earthy dance,
We grow more bold, we take a chance.

The moles are plotting, digging deep,
While squirrels above just plan to sweep.
We'll throw a party, mud pies galore,
And sing of fun from underground's core.

A carrot dreams of being a star,
While radishes think it's gone too far.
They throw a bash for all to see,
To celebrate the dirt-party spree.

So toast the soil, where friendships bloom,
With laughter ringing through the gloom.
From below we'll rise with our cheer,
With playful joy, we persevere!

The Power of Persistence

A tiny seed just wants to grow,
But finds the asphalt stealing the show.
It wiggles and squirms, needs room to slide,
Determined to make the concrete divide.

A gust of wind, a little rain,
To be a flower, there's much to gain.
With every push, it grins with pride,
As onlookers gather, eyes open wide.

A pigeon coos a melody sweet,
Encouragement from the park's heartbeat.
"Keep it up!" it chirps with flair,
And soon enough, blooms fill the air.

So here's to those who try and bend,
With laughter and grit, we make amends.
Out of the cracks, we boldly poke,
In life's grand joke, we play our stroke!

Shadows That Nurture

Under the shade of mighty trees,
Where acorns drop like peanut tease.
The little sprouts dance with delight,
Swaying and laughing in soft twilight.

The elder roots, they chuckle low,
"Just hang in there, watch us all grow!"
With jokes exchanged 'neath leafy bough,
They nurture dreams of the here and now.

A dandelion, quite out of place,
Winks and whispers, "Let's join the race!"
With laughter shared throughout the glade,
They bloom in shades that sunshine made.

In the depth of twilight, humor prevails,
With sprouts and shadows, no room for fails.
In every chuckle, there lies a spark,
For growth and joy that lights the dark!

Carved by Trials

Once a pebble thought it was grand,
Tumbled and bumbled over the land.
"Can't hold me down!" it jovially cried,
Each bump and bruise made it smile wide.

As rivers rushed with laughter clear,
The rocks around them held back fear.
"Come on!" they said, "Life's quite a game!
Let's dance with waves, let's make a name!"

Through valleys deep and hills so high,
The stone would chuckle as it flew by.
With trials met and stories spun,
It learned that fun comes second to none.

So here's to all who leap and roll,
Finding joy in each tiny hole.
Cracked but clever, we wear our scars,
With every tumble, we touch the stars!

The Ground We Tread

In the dirt where we play,
Wiggly weeds dance all day.
Beneath the surface, they thrive,
Cranky crabs groan, come alive.

Silly squirrels hold their feast,
On acorns of giant least.
While muddy boots stomp around,
In laughter, joy is found.

Untamed Resolve

In a jungle of tangled dreams,
The cactus blushes, so it seems.
"Prickly but proud," they squeak,
"Laughs bloom loud, though we're unique!"

The banana peels take their stand,
Slipping boldly all unplanned.
With a wink and twist, they slide,
Victory found in joy, not pride.

Emerald Fortitude

A sprout in a hat, what a sight,
Wiggly worms dance in delight.
With minty hopes and cherry cheer,
They tease the sun, bright and clear.

The broccoli wears a crown of greens,
While peas play hopscotch in the scenes.
"Veggies unite!" they boldly shout,
In their laughter, there's no doubt.

Persistent Petals

The daisies giggle in the breeze,
Tickling bees with subtle tease.
"More honey!" shouts the bold sunflower,
As petals swirl about the hour.

The dandelions wear their frowns,
While blowing wishes all around.
"Just don't chase us, we insist,
Or you'll find us in your wrist!"

Deep-Set Dreams

In the garden of oddities, plants may sway,
With dreams that sprout, as weeds often play.
My cucumber's laughing, it's five feet tall,
While tomatoes debate, who'll dance at the ball.

They whisper of sunshine, and hope they'll sprout,
But I'm here with my shovel, ready to pout.
With roots in the mud and worms in the mix,
Who knew gardening might lead to such tricks?

The carrots boast colors, a riotous show,
While beans twist like dancers, all in a row.
Through battles with pests and watering woes,
I chuckle at failures, as nature just blows.

So let's tip our hats to the plants that amuse,
With leafy shenanigans, nature's own dues.
With laughter we nurture, through dirt and through grime,

In the comedy of gardens, we flourish in prime.

Climbing Toward the Sun

There's a cactus named Spike, who dreams of a hug,
With arms made of needles, snug as a bug.
He waits for each traveler, eyeing them keen,
For a share of their sunshine, if they know what I mean.

Onions in layers, they cry out for fun,
While garlic just chuckles, 'Oh, we're number one!'
Up above the veggies, a mighty tall corn,
Winks down at the beet, since the day he was born.

Potatoes underground play hide and seek,
In a world of jest, they giggle and peek.
Though no one can see them, they have all the cheer,
For they know in their hearts, the sunshine is near!

So let's dance in the soil, embrace all the quirks,
From sprouts to the roots, through laughter it works.
With glee we'll all rise, like plants in the shade,
In a comedy garden, where fun's never weighed.

The Silent Testament

In the bustling earth, echoes of quiet cheer,
The mushrooms are plotting, secrets we hear.
While ants march in sync, each functioning cell,
Gossiping softly, it's quite the tableau!

The oak tree stands tall with a grin in its bark,
While squirrels tell tales of adventures in dark.
Hauling acorn treasures, they dash without sleep,
While the wise old tree chuckles, 'You're in too deep!'

Beneath the green canopy, giggles abound,
From pollen to petals, it's pure joy unbound.
With laughter on breezes that tickle the face,
The flora conspire, to share their sweet grace.

Let's raise a toast to the quiet camaraderie,
Of gardens and giggles, all wild and free.
From whispers of leaves to the chirps of the crowd,
The silent testament stands up, oh so proud.

Nourished by Struggle

In the patch where the wildflowers fight for their place,
The tulips and daisies all share in the race.
With roots intertwined, they tussle and twirl,
While the dandelions vote, 'Let's give it a whirl!'

The broccoli's flexing, trying to boast,
While cabbages giggle, claiming they're toast.
But oh, what a sight, as they dance through the rain,
Singing, 'Here comes the sunshine, let's grow once again!'

Through thorns and through thickets, the brambles all cheer,
While sunflowers beckon, the sky's drawing near.
Heroes in soil, with laughter their shield,
They bloom through their battles, never to yield.

So here's to the garden, where struggles get fun,
They thrive through the chaos, each under the sun.
With chuckles and joy, they show us their might,
In the dance of the lilies, it's pure delight!

Threads of Continuity

In a garden so wild and vast,
A flower once thought stuck in the past.
It danced with a breeze, felt quite spry,
Told squirrels, "I can reach for the sky!"

A worm claimed the soil was its throne,
Said, "Who needs legs when you've got your own?"
It wriggled with pride, a tiny brigade,
While beetles debated which shade they should trade!

A patch of grass grinned, said, "Look at me!"
"With no plans at all, I still look like glee!"
But every time it tried to stand tall,
It flopped like a clown—what a comical fall!

As butterflies giggled, the sun set low,
The garden, a circus, put on quite the show.
With laughter and quirks that filled the space,
Even roots laughed aloud at their own funny race!

Under the Canopy

Beneath leaves that flutter like a fan,
Lies a squirrel with a well-laid plan.
"I'll stash my nuts high!" it boldly declared,
Then forgot where they were, feeling quite scared!

A wise old owl hooted, "Keep your cool!"
"These woods are chaotic; just play it a tool!"
But the rabbit hopped by and tripped on a twig,
Said, "I'm just running away from a gig!"

In the shade where the shadows play games,
A grasshopper boasted of acrobatic claims.
But every jump ended with a loud thud,
Leaving all critters discussing his 'flood'!

Yet through all the tumbles, the giggles arose,
For nature's own chaos was truly the prose.
With a hint of a glide, a wink, and a cheer,
Life under the canopy was joyfully clear!

Seasons of Survival

When winter arrived with a frosty tease,
The bear nestled tight, dreaming of cheese.
While the mice threw a party, they had quite the spread,
"Just pass me the cheese and leave out the bread!"

In spring with the blossoms, a frog found his groove,
Croaking a tune with quite a smooth move.
But the dance floor got crowded, his ego did swell,
Until he slipped on a lily—oh, what a fell!

Summer brought sun, and the ants got to work,
While the lazy sloth thought, "What's the perk?"
He lounged on a leaf, dozing through the day,
And forgot he had plans; what a silly display!

As fall came a-calling, with colors so loud,
The raccoon wore masks, attempting to be proud.
He squeaked, "I'm in disguise, can you tell?
I'm a sneaky old bandit—it's going quite well!"

Through every season, hilarity spun,
In the game of survival, all needed some fun.
With laughs echoing wide in nature's own show,
It's clear that existence is best when we glow!

The Heart's Haven

In a nook of green, where daisies peek,
Lies a snail on a journey, a tad meek.
He sighed, "Oh dear, life moves so slow,
But I make the best trails; take that, you crow!"

A hedgehog rolled by, all prickles and pride,
Said, "I've got defense; you can't take my ride!"
But when dusk fell and shadows grew sly,
He squeaked, "Where's my blanket? Oh why, oh why!"

Beneath twinkling stars, a firefly glowed,
Telling tales of adventures wherever it strode.
"Last week I almost flew into a fly's soup!"
Which sent all the bugs into laughter-filled whoops!

The night sang with whispers, a warming embrace,
In their own little hearts, they each found a space.
For laughter and love made this haven divine,
Turned struggles to jokes—a design so fine!

The Tapestry of Tenacity

In a garden full of weeds, no rose should fret,
They grow a bit sideways, but don't give up yet.
With each twist and turn, they strike a funny pose,
Laughing at the problems, like a child with a hose.

The sun shines bright on their little green heads,
While squirrels toss acorns like they're hearty breads.
With a wink and a grin, they hold their own ground,
Making jokes with the wind, oh what fun can be found!

They juggle with raindrops, have dance-offs with breeze,
While dreaming of sunny days filled with cheese.
Each leaf has a story, some sillier than most,
But in the end, it's joy, that they love to boast.

So here's to the flowers, with their clumsy ballet,
Invisible battles in their own funny way.
With laughter as their shield, they rise with a cheer,
In their quirky ensemble, nothing to fear.

A Dance with Adversity

When storms roll in, they don't run for cover,
They throw on some rain boots, ready to discover.
A little mudslide turns into a game,
Splashing in puddles, shouting their fame.

With each gust of wind, they spin round and round,
Two-step with a tree, they dance on the ground.
While clouds look ominous, they bring out the fun,
Crafting umbrellas into hats, one by one.

They hold a parade with the squirrels in tow,
Feathers and leaves make their costumes aglow.
Chasing the troubles that seem to weigh down,
With humor in hearts, they flip doubts around.

So let laughter resound 'neath a gray swirling sky,
These brave little darlings refuse to say die.
When trouble comes knocking, they answer with glee,
In a dance with the winds, oh so carefree!

Beyond the Grind

In the midst of the chaos, they wiggle and squirm,
Finding a way to chill, unfazed by the term.
With silly expressions and a laughable twist,
They tackle the grind with a slapstick assist.

While others complain about the weight on their backs,
They ride it like horses, spurring up tracks.
With donuts for wheels, and giggles for gears,
They zoom past the frowns and ignore all the jeers.

They plant little flags made from socks in a chair,
To claim some new territory, what's for dinner, who cares?
Juggling their tasks with an old rubber band,
They tickle the stress, making humor their brand.

So when life takes a swing, they swing right back,
With laughter and pranks, they've got quite the knack.
Beyond the grindstone, they dash through the day,
Proving joy is the best, come what may!

Holding Fast in Turmoil

When storms make a racket, they're right in the fray,
Sipping lemonade as the clouds go gray.
A dance on the deck in their raincoats so bright,
They just giggle along, bringing joy to the night.

While others are fretting, pacing back and forth,
They set up a party, giving chaos its worth.
Pinatas are popping, confetti's a must,
Laughing at trouble, in fun they trust.

While the world is spinning like tops out of whack,
They wobble and chuckle, never losing their track.
With marshmallows flying, they fortify cheer,
Building castles of laughter, oh what a frontier!

So when life gets rocky, with hurdles galore,
They put on their clown shoes and settle the score.
In the midst of the turmoil, they shine like a gem,
Hanging tight, side by side, just laughing at them!

www.ingramcontent.com/pod-product-compliance
Lightning Source LLC
Chambersburg PA
CBHW071814160426
43209CB00003B/77